Hannah Farley-Hills for HFH Productions Limited
in association with Neil McPherson for the Finborough Theatre
presents

The world premiere

FOAL

by Titas Halder

Foal premiered at the Finborough Theatre, London,
on Tuesday, 5 May 2026.

FOAL

by Titas Halder

Cast
A.K.   **Amar Chadha-Patel**

The running time is approximately 90 minutes.

There will be no interval.

Director   **Annie Kershaw**
Set and Costume Designer   **Cara Evans**
Lighting Designer   **Rajiv Pattani**
Composer and Sound Designer   **Pierre Flasse**
Casting Consultant   **Becky Paris CDG**
Production Manager   **Nick Flintoff**
Stage Manager   **Ciara O'Neill**
Assistant Director   **Jillian Feuerstein**
Producer   **Hannah Farley-Hills**

Please see front of house notices or ask an usher for an exact running time.

Please note that performances may begin up to five minutes later than the advertised start time as latecomers cannot be admitted while the performance is in progress.

Please turn your mobile phones off – the light they emit can be distracting.

Our patrons are respectfully reminded that, in this intimate theatre, any noise such as the rustling of programmes, talking or the ringing of mobile phones may distract the actors and your fellow audience members.

We regret there is no admittance or re-admittance to the auditorium whilst the performance is in progress.

Amar Chadha-Patel | A.K.
Amar Chadha-Patel will next appear in the feature film *Motor City* which premiered at last year's Venice International Film Festival, and can currently be seen in the historical epic *William Tell*.

On television, he stars in the Netflix Limited series *The Decameron* as well as in the Lucasfilm for Disney+ show *Willow*, based on the cult classic Ron Howard film.

Other credits include Gareth Edwards' *The Creator*, the Independent Spirit Award nominated *Slip*, the male lead in the feature *Dashcam*, and *The Third Day* for HBO and Sky.

Titas Halder | Playwright
Playwright Titas Halder returns to the Finborough Theatre which saw his playwriting debut with *Run the Beast Down* in 2017 (also seen at the Marlowe Theatre, Canterbury, and Strawdog Theatre, Chicago). He is currently Associate Artistic Director at the Donmar Warehouse.

As a writer he trained on the Royal Court Theatre Young Writers' Programme. His first two plays saw him nominated for Best Writer at the inaugural The Stage Debut Awards; his next play *The Basement* was a finalist for the Verity Bargate Award. Plays include *Replica* (National Theatre Connections and Länk Festival Riksteatern, Stockholm) and *Escape the Scaffold* (Theatre503 and The Other Room, Cardiff). He was part of BBC Voices 2024 and is currently writing his first feature film for Storyteller. As a director, his work includes *King Lear* (Sheffield Crucible), *The Lemon Table* – co-directed with Michael Grandage (Salisbury Playhouse and UK tour), *A Boy and His Soul* (Kiln Theatre) and *The Dance of Death* (Donmar Trafalgar). Titas also performs and records as musical artist Titas and the Fox.

Annie Kershaw | Director
Annie Kershaw was the 2024 winner of the Genesis Future Directors Award at the Young Vic. In 2026, she was shortlisted for the Arts Foundation Futures Award for Theatre Directing. Annie was the 2023-2024 Carne Deputy Director at Jermyn Street Theatre.

Direction include *Girl In the Machine* and *Light* (Young Vic), *The Maids* (Jermyn Street Theatre), *Educating Rita* and *Hedda Gabler* (Reading Rep Theatre), *Private View* (Soho Theatre). Associate and Assistant Direction includes *Juniper*

Blood (Donmar Warehouse), *Best of Enemies* (Noël Coward Theatre and Young Vic), *Jekyll and Hyde* and *Dorian* (Reading Rep Theatre) and *Henry II* (Rabble Theatre).

Cara Evans | Set and Costume Designer
Cara Evans (They/She) is a London-based designer.
Trained in Design for Stage at the Royal Central School of Speech and Drama.
Designs include *Sleepova* and *Statues* (Bush Theatre), *Dear Young Monster* (Bristol Old Vic and Soho Theatre), *Ugly Sisters* (New Diorama Theatre and Soho Theatre), *Body Show* (Soho Theatre), *Dynolwaith* (Sherman Theatre, Cardiff), *The Living Newspaper* and *Queer Upstairs* (Royal Court Theatre), *Wish You Were Here* (Gate Theatre), *Get Dressed!* (Unicorn Theatre), *Feral Monster* (Welsh National Theatre), *Educating Rita* (Reading Rep Theatre), *Sylvia* (English Theatre Frankfurt), *It's a Motherf**king Pleasure* (International Tour), *Millennium Girls* (Brixton House Theatre), *The Maladies* (Kiln Theatre), *Sirens* (Mercury Theatre, Colchester), *SK Shlomo Breathe* (Royal Albert Hall), *F**king Men* (Waterloo East Theatre), *The Beach House* (Park Theatre), *GRILLS* (Camden People's Theatre), *Love Bomb* (National Youth Theatre), *Baba Joon* (Swansea Grand Theatre), *Bright Half Life* (King's Head Theatre), *The Misandrist* (Arcola Theatre) and *Instructions for A Teenage Armageddon* (Southwark Playhouse).
Associate Designs include *Teenage Dick* (Donmar Warehouse Schools Tour).

Rajiv Pattani | Lighting Designer
Productions at the Finborough Theatre include *£1 Thursdays*.
Theatre includes *What Fatima Did* (Tara Theatre), *Comedy Of Errors Remixed* (Intermission Youth Theatre and Courtyard Theatre), *Twelfth Night* (Tabard Theatre and Thèâtre Du Passage, Switzerland), *Brown Girl Noise* (Riverside Studios), *The Walrus Has A Right To Adventure* (Everyman Theatre, Liverpool), *In Search Of Goldoni* and *Sorry, You're Not a Winner* (Bristol Old Vic Theatre and Theatre Royal, Plymouth), *Heisenberg* and *Some Demon* (Arcola Theatre), *Elmer Adventure* (The Lowry, Salford, Southbank Centre, London and National Tour), *The Society For New Cuisine* and *10 Nights* (Omnibus Theatre), *Alice in Wonderland* and *Kabul Goes Pop: Music Television Afghanistan* (Brixton House), *Peanut Butter and Blueberries* (Kiln Theatre), *Test Match, The Maladies, Yellowman, Statements After an Arrest Under the Immortality Act,* and *OUTSIDE* (Orange Tree Theatre, Richmond), *Strategic Love Play* (Soho Theatre, Edinburgh Fringe Festival and International Tour), *The Garden of Words* (Park Theatre) and *Wolfie* (Theatre503).

Pierre Flasse | Composer and Sound Designer
Pierre is a composer, sound designer and theatre maker based in London. Trained at the University of Manchester.
He is the composer's assistant to Sally Potter OBE, and, as a multi-instrumentalist, he has performed around the UK in genres spanning jazz to Indian folk.
Composition and Sound Designs include *Iphigenia In Aulis* (Bloomsbury Theatre), *Limp Wrist and the Iron Fist* (Brixton House Theatre), *Fanny* (King's Head Theatre), *Nostos: After The Odyssey* (Southwark Playhouse Borough) *Permission* (Tara Theatre), *Miraculous* (Old Red Lion Theatre), *Frat* (Prague Fringe, Brighton Fringe,

Camden Fringe and Edinburgh Festival Fringe), *Local* (Northern Tour), *BIG STRONG MAN* (Northern Tour), *Pillock* (Edinburgh Festival Fringe and Shakespeare North Playhouse), *Joy Unspeakable* (Northern Tour), *Seed to Soil* (The Lowry, Salford) and *The Bell Curves* (Contact Theatre, Manchester). Assistant Sound Designs include *Piaf and Pinocchio* (Watermill Theatre, Newbury).

Associate Sound Designs include *The Ladies Football Club* (Crucible Theatre, Sheffield), *Factory* (Royal Shakespeare Company Next Gen), *Julius Caesar* (Orange Tree Theatre, Richmond) and *The Snow Queen* (Reading Rep Theatre).

Becky Paris CDG | Casting Consultant
Becky is currently Head of Casting at Shakespeare's Globe where she has cast over fifty productions for the Globe Theatre and Sam Wanamaker Playhouse. She is also a freelance Casting Director who has worked on theatre projects for Headlong, Almeida Theatre, NT Studios, ATG, Park Theatre, Southwark Theatre, Hampstead Theatre, Pentabus, HighTide and Sheffield Theatres, as well as a number of short films. Recent work for Shakespeare's Globe includes *Mother Courage and Her Children*, *Love's Labour's Lost*, *Much Ado About Nothing*, *As You Like It*, *Pinocchio*, *Deep Azure*, *The Tempest*, *A Midsummer Night's Dream*, *Romeo and Juliet*, *The Crucible*, *Troilus and Cressida*, *All's Well That Ends Well*, *Cymbeline*, *Three Sisters*, *Antony and Cleopatra*, *Princess Essex*, *Ghosts*, *Othello* and *The Duchess of Malfi*.
Other theatre includes *Robota* (Headlong), *Welcome to Pemfort* (Soho Theatre), *A Ghost In Your Ear* (Hampstead Theatre), *Ragdoll* (Jermyn Street Theatre), *The House Party* and *A View From the Bridge* (National Tours for Headlong), *Hir* (Park Theatre), *Brilliant Jerks* (Southwark Playhouse) and *Anna X* (VAULT Festival).

Nick Flintoff | Production Manager
Trained at RADA and studied documentary film at The Metropolitan Film School. He currently works as a freelance Production Manager and Filmmaker. He has worked all over the world as a Production Manager for Imagination Ltd. and later worked at the National Theatre for ten years in their New Work Department as Technical and Production Manager, developing new work for the main stages and other national theatres. More recently, Nick was the Technical and Production Manager for the Watermill Theatre, Newbury, where he worked on the award-winning musical revival of *The Lord Of The Rings*, and the hugely successful *A Ghost In Your Ear* (Hampstead Theatre). www.nickflintoff.com.

Ciara O'Neill | Stage Manager
Trained in BA Theatre and Drama Studies at Munster Technological University.
Theatre includes *The Witches of Eastwick* (Bernie Grant Arts Centre), *The Sad Panto* (Cork Arts Theatre), *The 25th Annual Putnam County Spelling Bee* (Rory Gallagher Theatre, Cork) and *Earthquakes in London* (Stack Theatre).

Jillian Feuerstein | Assistant Director
Productions at the Finborough Theatre (where she is Resident Assistant Director) include Associate Director on *Diagnosis*, and Assistant Director on *The Truth About Blayds*. Trained on the MFA in Contemporary Directing Practice at Rose Bruford College.
Direction includes *The Story* (Rose Theatre), *Women of Will* (Barn

Theatre) and *Revolt. She Said. Revolt Again.* (Rose Bruford Studios). Assistant Direction includes assisting Abigail Graham on *Trueman and the Arsonists* (Roundhouse) and Walter Meierjohann on *Machinal* (RADA Studios).

Hannah Farley-Hills for HFH Productions | Producer

HFH Productions is an independent producer of award-winning work, run by Hannah Farley-Hills. The company develops, mounts and tours theatrical productions that showcase underrepresented perspectives and untested ideas. Hannah believes a good play leaves you with more questions than it answers, things you should still be questioning in a week, a month, a year.

Hannah's recent productions include *A Ghost In Your Ear* by Jamie Armitage, created in collaboration with Ben and Max Ringham (Hampstead Theatre), the multi award-winning *Bacon* by Sophie Swithinbank which originally began at the Finborough Theatre (YES24 Theatre in Seoul, Soho Playhouse in New York, Bristol Old Vic, and Summerhall as part of the Edinburgh Fringe Festival, and Riverside Studios), *Dear Annie, I Hate You* by Sam Ipema (Riverside Studios and Pleasance Edinburgh), and the award-winning *Surrender* by Sophie Swithinbank (Arcola Theatre and Summerhall, Edinburgh).

Other notable HFH shows include *Flicker* by Gabriella Foley (Pleasance Edinburgh), *C Is For Clown* and *Better Together* by ACA Theatre (National tour and international pilot, Chile), *...If We've Never Been to the Moon?* and *The Naughty Fox* by James Baldwin (National tour).

Hannah was previously Associate Producer to international production company, Glynis Henderson Productions, working on Fix + Foxy's critically acclaimed international production, *Dark Noon*, Associate Producer to London new writing company, Arch 468, and a Projects Producer at The Marlowe, Canterbury. Hannah is a recipient of the Stage One Producer bursary, an MGCfutures bursary and is a member of the League of Independent Producers. Hannah is also Executive Director of early years and disability specialist theatre company, Toucan Theatre.

www.hfh.productions

'**Probably the most influential fringe theatre in the world.**'
Time Out

'**Not just a theatre, but a miracle.**' *Metro*

'**The mighty little Finborough which, under Neil McPherson, continues to offer a mixture of neglected classics and new writing in a cannily curated mix.**'
Lyn Gardner, *The Stage*

'**The tiny but mighty Finborough.**'
Ben Brantley, *The New York Times*

Founded in 1980, the multi-award-winning Finborough Theatre presents plays and music theatre, concentrated exclusively on vibrant new writing and unique rediscoveries – both in our 1868 Victorian home and online with our digital initiative – #FinboroughFrontier – including *Remember Your Lovers – The Poetry of Sidney Keyes*, a poetry recital of one of England's greatest Second World War poets, starring Claire Bloom, and available wherever you get your podcasts.

Our programme is unique – we never present work that has had a full run in London during the last 25 years. Behind the scenes, we continue to discover and develop a new generation of theatre makers. Despite remaining completely unsubsidised, the Finborough Theatre has an unparalleled track record for attracting the finest talent who go on to become leading voices in British theatre. Under Artistic Director Neil McPherson, it has discovered some of the UK's most exciting new playwrights including Laura Wade, James Graham, Mike Bartlett, Jack Thorne, Athena Stevens and Anders Lustgarten, and directors including Tamara Harvey, Robert Hastie, Tom Littler, Blanche McIntyre, Kate Wasserberg and Sam Yates.

In the 1990s, the Finborough Theatre first became known for new writing including Naomi Wallace's first play *The War Boys*, Rachel Weisz in David Farr's *Neville Southall's Washbag*, four plays by Anthony Neilson including *Penetrator* and *The Censor*, both of which transferred to the Royal Court Theatre.

New writing development included the premieres of modern classics such as Mark Ravenhill's *Shopping and F***king*, Conor McPherson's *This Lime Tree Bower*, Naomi Wallace's *Slaughter City* and Martin McDonagh's *The Pillowman*.

Since 2000, new British plays have included Laura Wade's London debut *Young Emma* (commissioned by the Finborough Theatre), James Graham's London debut *Albert's Boy* with Victor Spinetti and four of his first plays, Sarah Grochala's *S27*, Athena Stevens' *Schism* which was nominated for an Olivier Award, and West End transfers for Joy Wilkinson's *Fair*, Nicholas de

Jongh's *Plague Over England*, Jack Thorne's *Fanny and Faggot*, Neil McPherson's Olivier Award nominated *It Is Easy To Be Dead*, and Dawn King's *Foxfinder*.

UK premieres of foreign plays have included plays by Lanford Wilson, Larry Kramer, Tennessee Williams, Suzan-Lori Parks, the English premieres of two Scots language classics by Robert McLellan, and more Canadian plays than any other theatre in Europe, with West End transfers for Frank McGuinness' *Gates of Gold* with William Gaunt, Craig Higginson's *Dream of the Dog* with Dame Janet Suzman, and Jordan Tannahill's *Late Company*. In December 2022, *Pussycat in Memory of Darkness* was the first play performed by a foreign theatre in Ukraine since the Russian invasion.

Rediscoveries of neglected work – most commissioned by the Finborough Theatre – have included the first London revivals of Rolf Hochhuth's *Soldiers* and *The Representative*, both parts of Keith Dewhurst's *Lark Rise to Candleford*, *Etta Jenks* with Clarke Peters, three rediscoveries from Noël Coward, Terence Rattigan's *Variation On A Theme* with Rachael Stirling, and Lennox Robinson's *Drama at Inish* with Celia Imrie and Paul O'Grady. Transfers have included Emlyn Williams' *Accolade*, John Van Druten's *London Wall*, and J. B. Priestley's *Cornelius* which had a sell-out Off-Broadway run in New York City.

Music Theatre has included West End transfers for Adam Gwon's *Ordinary Days* and the UK premiere of Rodgers and Hammerstein's *State Fair*. Playlists of Finborough Theatre music theatre are available to listen to for free on Spotify.

The Finborough Theatre won the 2020 and 2022 *London Pub Theatres* Pub Theatre of the Year Award, *The Stage* Fringe Theatre of the Year Award in 2011 and nominated in 2026, the Empty Space Peter Brook Award in 2010 and 2012 and nominated in 2023 and 2024, and was nominated for an Olivier Award in 2017 and 2019. Artistic Director Neil McPherson was awarded the Critics' Circle Special Award for Services to Theatre in 2019. It is the only non-public funded theatre ever to be awarded the Channel 4 Playwrights Scheme bursary twelve times.
www.finboroughtheatre.co.uk

Production Acknowledgements

Artwork Photography	**Sari Soininen**
Artwork Design and Digital Graphic Design	**Ellie Farley-Hills**
Filmmaker	**Pip Films**
Press Representation	**Kate Morley PR**
Set Builder	**Brett Orzel for Fraktl**

The production would like to thank Caitlin Laing-McEvoy on the Baritone Sax, White Light, The Albany, Brixton House, and Tara Theatre.

And with special thanks to Jon and NoraLee Sedmak, and Stage One.

Mailing
Email **admin@finboroughtheatre.co.uk** or give your details to our Box
Office staff to join our free email list.

Playscripts
Many of the Finborough Theatre's plays have been published and are on sale
from our website.

Sustainability
The Finborough Theatre has a 100% sustainable electricity supply, has
replaced single-use plastic glasses with paper, and no longer uses paper
tickets.

30andUnder programme
Our 30andUnder programme offers multiple benefits for younger
theatregoers. Sign up through our website.

Safeguarding
Everyone is welcome and respected at the Finborough Theatre.
There is no place for any form of discrimination or harassment here. If you
experience or witness anything that makes you uncomfortable, please speak to
a member of staff or email us at **admin@finboroughtheatre.co.uk**

Local History
The Finborough Theatre's local history website is online at
www.earlscourtlocalhistory.co.uk

Programming Funds
The Finborough Theatre New Writing Fund and the Finborough Theatre
Rediscoveries Fund allows you to directly support the areas of theatre
you most want to see – vibrant new writing, or unique rediscoveries.
Contact us at **development@finboroughtheatre.co.uk**

Friends of the Finborough Theatre
The Finborough Theatre is a registered charity. We receive no public
funding, and rely solely on the support of our audiences.
Please do consider supporting us by joining our Friends of the Finborough
Theatre scheme.
There are five categories of Friends, each offering a wide range of benefits.
Please ask any member of our staff for a leaflet.
William Terriss Friends – Anonymous. Iain Clarke. Fiona Clements. Tim
Doyle. Anne and Patrick Foster. Kenita Garffus. Stephen Godfrey. Ros and Alan
Haigh. Melinda Patton. Chris Rocker. Linda Thorson.
James Bohee Friends – Stephen Joseph, Janet and Leo Liebster, Ann and
Richard Lienard. Catrin Evans. Kate Howe. Paul and Nicolette Kirkby.
Adelaide Neilson Friends – Charles Glanville. Philip G Hooker.
Legacy Gifts – Tom Erhardt. Mike Frohlich.

Smoking is not permitted in the auditorium.
The videotaping or making of electronic or other audio and/or visual recordings of this production is strictly prohibited.
There is no admittance or readmittance into the auditorium whilst the performance is in progress.

In accordance with the requirements of the Royal Borough of Kensington and Chelsea:
1. The public may leave at the end of the performance by all doors and such doors must at that time be kept open.
2. All gangways, corridors, staircases and external passageways intended for exit shall be left entirely free from obstruction whether permanent or temporary.
3. Persons shall not be permitted to stand or sit in any of the gangways intercepting the seating or to sit in any of the other gangways.
4. No drinks, containing intoxicating liquor or not, shall be consumed within the auditorium unless supplied in plastic, wax paper or cardboard containers.
5. No bottles or cans shall be permitted in the auditorium.

FOAL

Titas Halder

Acknowledgements

Thanks to
Nikesh Patel, Sachin K Sharma,
Neil McPherson and the Finborough Theatre,
Jon and NoraLee Sedmak,
Kara Fitzpatrick,
Liz Bacon,
and the sensational trio
Amar Chadha-Patel, Annie Kershaw, Hannah Farley-Hills.

4

Please tick one box

[ ] British (White)

[ ] BAME

[ ] Paki

[ ] Indian

[ ] Fuck you, motherfucker.

Character

A play for one actor.

A.K., *British Asian, thirties*

Notes

A simple stage.

Something always happens in a *Pause*.

A *Beat* is more for rhythm.

Silence means the words have run out.

Sometimes within dialogue I used bold, italics, and underlined words for (different types of) emphasis. And even sometimes I'll do weird stuff like < this! > .

Hopefully any stage directions, also in italics, are clear from context.

The approach to capitalisations and other points of grammar (line-breaks, full stops, dashes) are about rhythm and flow and reflect the idiosyncrasies of the storyteller.

This text went to press before the end of rehearsals and so may differ slightly from the play as performed.

do-wel and have wel
and God shal have thi soule
and do yvel and have yvel
hope thow noon other
but after thi deeth day
the devel shal have thi soule

'Piers Plowman'
William Langland, 14th C.

PART I

THE SEA

1. Mowgli

There is always a song in my head.
Ever since I was little, as long as I can remember
There has *always* been music
When I wake up
When I go to bed
Melodies, little tunes
Spill out
At night when I'm trying to sleep
It soothes me
Without music
I'd become feral
If it stopped
I don't know who I'd be.

Silence.

Waves lap
Black blood in moonlight
I don't regret what I did.
It was the right thing to do.

He starts again.

In the playground, there were two games of football. The older
kids, and the younger kids. Our school was surrounded on all
sides by houses – kick the ball over the fence and you're done.
Game over. We had a strip by the side of the classroom, and the
older boys had a pitch on the tarmac. Max was in our year – but
he was so good he was allowed in the older kids' game.

Midflow, world cup final. Brazil versus England. I was
Romário. We were losing 3-1. For a moment, our game spilled

into their game, my best friend Harry kicked our ball onto their pitch. Max ran straight over, knocked him down, sent him flying – then booted our ball miles over the wall. End of game. Fuck knows if we were ever gonna get it back. It was a fresh one as well, no chunks hacked out of the sponge. Harry picked himself up, pink in the face, on the verge of tears. I was livid. Without thinking, I ran into their game, nicked their ball and smashed it over.

Beat.

Max's face. He literally saw red – his face was bright pink, puffed up like he was having an allergic reaction. Panting, hair straggling across his forehead, he couldn't believe it. His eyes were bulging. He was big. I was small. Skinny, ribcage like a skeleton. Terrible mistake. Immediate regret. He charged at me like a bull, shoved me to the ground. My head smacked the concrete. He stood over me. I braced myself. Mr. Harrison swooped in and swung him away. As I got up, everyone was standing round me. Looking at me like a hero. Charlotte Bailey smiled at me. I went bright red.

He smiles.

When I got home, Mum and Dad were pissed off at me. Not cos I'd hurt Max, I couldn't have. Not cos of the hole in my trousers (although that did also piss mum off). But because the school *sent a letter home*. The *idea* of getting into trouble was worse than the reality – it brought embarrassment, *shame* to their doorstep. And that was the worst thing you could do. Bring shame. But you could bring shame upon the family for the smallest thing. Girlfriend? Shame upon the family. Smoking? Shame upon the family. Drugs? Out the house. Gay? – you're dead.

But Max started it. I dobbed him in unashamed. Dad looked up their number in the phone book and asked them to come over and apologise. Fuck. I stood in the driveway while they sorted it out. Me and Max hung about in the background, kicked a ball around. Max's Dad was calm, respectful even. He made Max say sorry. Then Dad turned to me –

Say you're sorry too.

No.

Max's Dad played it down – didn't mind. But my Dad was
fuming. He went inside, slammed the door. For a minute I
thought that was it. But then Max's Dad pulled me round the
side of the house. Backed me up against the brick.

If you ever humiliate my son again
I will take a can of petrol
pour it through your letter box
and set fire to your house.
I will kill you and your fucking family.

He glared at Max

And *you* –
Wait till I get you home.

As they walked off down the driveway, Max picked up a stone
and threw it at our car. The window shattered into tiny little
squares of glass.

Pause.

There was another me, inside
Who wanted to cry
He had a thick lump stuck in his throat
I ignored him, buried him deep.

Pause.

Be careful, Mum and Dad would say
Be careful
They're out there looking for you

*

11.
I grew up on an Island.
There was one other Asian boy at my school – Raj.
And of course I wouldn't have thought about it at the time but
Maybe he was more *Indian* than me
not that I think of myself as that – I'm English

But maybe his family were a bit more traditional or
Stuck
Because he was less *knowing* of the world he was in or
More trusting maybe
He was harmless, never stood out
But for some reason The Headmistress singled him out-
She made him stand up in front of everyone
And called him *Mowgli*.

Stop showing off.
If you don't behave
I'll make you pull your trousers down right here.

Everyone laughed
I laughed – it was funny.
He was upset – I could see it in his face
I didn't care.
Because *I* had escaped.
He looked ashamed
Like he'd done something wrong.
She strutted around like she'd delivered justice.
He was Mowgli.
Not me.

2. Break-In

What would you do if you were attacked in your home?

Pause.

Everyone has deranged violent fantasies –
Don't they.

Beat.

About what they'd do if someone broke in –

I've got a baseball bat under my bed.
Krav Maga, roundhouse to the face.
Dhalsim mate. Street Fighter II Turbo

Knock them the fuck out.

But in reality, you don't know what you'd do until it happens –
until it's happening and you've got no choice.

Summer holidays, back from uni. I had become nocturnal. Mum
and Dad were out at work, my sister was at school. No cars in
the driveway. I always thought that break-ins happened when it
was dark. Turns out the best time to rob a house is in the middle
of the day.

3am. ITV2+1. Taxi Driver / Apocalypse Now back to back.
Don't know what time I went to bed. The next day I got up *late*.
Fell out of a dream. I was in the shower, music in my head. I
got out, heard footsteps on the stairs. My brain thought *it's Dad,
back from work*. I came out the bathroom in my pants, crossed
the landing, leant over the bannisters and there on his way up,
was a kid – baseball cap and kappa tracksuit – same age as me.
And this is what I did –

Pause.

I *ran* **at** him.
Charged down the stairs.
He *bolted*, turned his back
Legged it into the living room
– shouted

DAD.

I arrived a second later,
burst through the door *in my pants*
to see the kid staring across at a wiry man
White, before you ask, in his forties
Screwdriver in one hand,
swiping our video camera with the other
This scabby-looking guy in the living room
The *father* of this fucking kid, *froze*
The three of us locked in a standoff
The boy, adrenaline blitzing through his veins
The *Dad*, scaghead, caught in the act
And me, fucking raging, standing *in my pants*.
The Dad came at me, screwdriver aimed at my neck

As he went to stab me in the throat
I barked a torrent of abuse

DROP THAT CAMERA YOU FUCKING PRICK
GET THE FUCK OUT OF THIS HOUSE
GET THE *FUCK OUT OF THIS HOUSE*
GET THE FUCK OUT YOU FUCKING CUNT.

Pause.

He stopped, startled. I was shaking.
He turned to go back the way they'd come in:
The kitchen window, smashed, in pieces on the floor
The kid tried to climb out but cut himself on the glass
The Dad screamed

STOP
You'll hurt yourself.

He climbed back down
and we were stuck again

My brain thought
he cares about him,
he doesn't want him to get hurt.
a father and son robbery team
– that is actually quite sweet.

Silence.

Don't move.
I'll open the front door.

I backed out of the room but the door was locked
I fumbled in the kitchen drawer to find the key
If they were going to attack me, this would be the time.
If they wanted to kill me, it would be now, and they'd win.
I got the door unlocked, flung it open
They flew past me, legged it down the drive
I slammed the door shut, sat on the stairs in shock.
A small thought crawled across my frontal lobe:
I ran into that room ready to fight.

It felt good.

To *know that about myself.*
What I didn't know
Was how angry it would make me
And sad.

Pause.

The other me wanted to call my Dad
Needed him to comfort me
This time, I listened.
Dad, can you come home?
Something's happened.

*

My Dad's a doctor
Ophthalmology.
Quiet, calm – peacemaker.
His whole department is Indian doctors
They all came to the Island at the same time
And they came here because the country needed them
Needed their skills, needed them to help build the NHS
Lest you fucking forget
They were invited.

Pause.

Before he retired,
he told me about a man who came in to have his cataracts done.

I'm glad, I'm very happy with the way things are going
Because there's too many immigrants here
But perhaps now, they might think twice.

I'm an immigrant.

No, not you
I don't mean you
People like you are alright

You're one of the good ones.

Dad carried out his duty of care
With impeccable skill and precision.

Pause.

I suppose the thing
that made me burn with rage
Is that it made my Dad sad.
I had seen him angry
I had seen him shout,
at me, at the news
But I had never seen him *sad.*

When I was seven we went to India
We rushed; it took days to get to the place
where his Father was dying.
We arrived a few hours too late.
I remember being stood in that room
With Mum, Dad, and a body on the table
of a man I'd never met – my Grandfather
I remember his skin, cold, clammy.
I remember that moment
and I don't remember him being sad then.
He was quiet. Stoic. Accepting.
But he was sad now,
hearing this man who he'd helped more than once
Speak utter shit out of his mouth
A man who said he respected my Dad
because he was a Doctor –
Who saw him as a *good* one
But hated the others.

Pause.

That was Max's Dad, Tony Barnes.
– He was a cunt.
So you can see, that Max was a cunt too.
We used to be friends for fuck's sake
Played football down the rec
But Max was a pathological liar
He made all sorts of shit up at school
Said he took an E every morning with his cornflakes
Tried to sell us his dad's Viagra but it was tic tacs
He said his dad taught him how to hot-wire a car –

They owned a garage down the hill
Barnes' Tyres –
Where everyone knew they sold heroin and crack
front yard covered with scrap
Shop mannequins, the decaying carcass of a Citroën 2CV
There was a rumour they bred illegal dogs
There was always this big beast chained up at the front of the
house
Sat outside slobbering;
There were stories about Max's Dad and his mates
Rob Dixon – Big Rob – proper skinhead; mechanic
Bully, a snake, beat up his own family
Everyone said he was National Front
And Gary Grindle, caretaker at the school, rat
Paedo, a predator who got a pupil pregnant
Everyone knew but no one did anything
Because it was the Island and no one gave a shit
It was a nowhere place
And if you stayed you weren't gonna get out.

Pause.

My Mum hated it – she would say things like
<u>I will be buried here on this Island against my will</u>

Like she was a character in a Victorian novel

Pause.

She would write me little letters of advice
Seal them in envelopes and leave them on my pillow

You have to be better than them
You have to try twice as hard
Because they won't listen to you
They won't respect you
You have to be relentless
You have to be hard of heart

Pause.

The Island seemed safe
But people could keep secrets then

Adults could hide their crimes
The press was obsessed with missing kids
So we grew up scared
Thinking we'd get abducted
On the way home from school
By the ice cream man or the music teacher
We were told to be silent.
What we needed was *care*.

Pause.

Mum didn't work. She stopped after I was born. Made sure I knew it was my fault. She was strict. Had a temper. But there was something else. Something beneath. Inherited. Irrational. – In year 10 I asked for a dog. I wanted a black lab. We would have been best friends. We had a garden. We could have walked on the beach. I would have cared for it so much. The first time I asked, she flipped. Repulsed at the thought.

They're filthy, dirty
You wouldn't take care of it.
You're not responsible.
You're not caring.
You're not kind.

Her eyes went black.
And she would turn.

Why should I give you what you want
– for nothing?
When I gave up everything for you.
Stopped working
Stayed at home
Because of you
Because of *you*
I didn't have a life.

Beat.

(Right
I didn't ask to be born
that's your mistake
not mine)

Pause.

After we argued I would go outside and climb into the hedge – a hole in the conifer where I could disappear. It was clear to me how much I disappointed them. I'm sure my Mum thought all her problems began when I was born. I know this because she would say to me *I was fine until you were born and then all my problems began.* Her catchphrase was

I'm going to call Social Services and have you taken away.

Pause.

That's not fair. There was tenderness. One day, when I was little, she came to collect me from nursery and found they had put me in a corner, penned me in alone while the other kids played together.

Why is he there?
There – in the corner?

He's sick.
He's got a temperature.
He was turning yellow.
I didn't want him to infect the other children.

If he's sick,
Why didn't you ring me?
Why didn't you call the doctor?

Pause.

Mum lifted me up in her arms and held me close.
She never brought me back.

Silence.

The day of the break-in, Mum got back home late. I was in the living room with Dad; he'd bought me fish and chips. I didn't tell either of them I'd been attacked, I couldn't. Mum stared at me, at the broken window.

Why didn't you clear it up?

She fetched the dustpan.

Got on her hands and knees.

Were you waiting for me to do it?
Why were you still in bed?
This is your fault.

Silence.

I wasn't what they wanted
I wasn't who they wanted
I wasn't going to be a doctor, lawyer, fucking pharmacist,
dentist
I wanted to be Sachin Tendulkar
I wanted to be Darren Gough
I wanted to be Shane Warne
I wanted to be Brian Lara

Pause.

I kept bothering her
About the dog
I could see it was winding her up
So I kept going
I didn't back down
I found it fun
I goaded her
baited her into a fight
Argued and argued until
One morning
I dunno how
I dunno why
I dunno what I said but
Out of nowhere
She threw the remote control at my face
It split the skin beside my eye socket
Cut me open
She didn't say a thing
I walked into school blood streaming down my face
None of the teachers did anything
I cleaned myself up at the back of the class in physics

I wanted to see Katy

I knew she would console me
I knew she'd care
She was the only one.
I'd see her at break
I felt the blood start to scab over
I couldn't wait.

3. True Love

Katy was my best friend. She didn't join in Year 7 with
everybody else, she came a year later from another school. I
was in awe. She was insanely clever, everyone fancied her,
she wasn't part of the popular crew, and incredibly, she liked
me – cos I was funny. See when you're short and a loser and
a bit fat you have to be funnier than everyone else. This is not
necessarily a funny story so you're not really seeing that part of
me. But it's true – undisputed Class Clown, est. 1987.

I knew Katy's phone number off by heart. I still do. I called her
landline every evening or she called mine. Didn't even care if
her mum or dad picked up.

Can I speak to Katy please?

Don't you think you call a lot?

We'd talk and talk and talk
About everything
For hours.
We talked until the battery died
Fuck the phone bill
I wasn't paying
We'd talk til it got dark
In bed, blankets over our heads, breathing
beside each other in silence – *Us*
The thrill of talking in secret under the covers
Sharing comfort, closeness

Always told each other the truth.
One day
We were saying goodnight
And she was silent
For a moment
And I could hear her there
And I could feel she wanted to say it

I care about you.

< !!! >

I care about you too
I'll always care about you.

Silence.

The day after Year 10 exams finished, a group of us went down
to the beach. It was windy, the sea was cold. Max was still a
cock, but he was friends with some of my friends. Someone
dared him to do a Tombstone.

When we were about 8, this boy Francis, the neighbours'
cousin, came down to visit from Wigan or something. His
cousins dared him as well. A tombstone is a blind vertical jump,
feet-first into the water. The tide was too low. Francis hit the
side of his head on a rock. Fractured his skull and shattered his
collar bone. He was pulled out of the water unconscious. Think
he got brain damage. Didn't come back the next year.

Max stood on the edge of the sea wall, fearless. Rough waves
beneath. You could see the rocks. This is how you break your
neck and drown. He jumped. Hit the water. Disappeared under
the swell. I looked over at Katy. She was rapt. He surfaced.
Flung his hair back.

FUCK YEAH

YEAH!

That evening Siobhan Jessop had a party. I wasn't allowed to
go because of my fucking parents. Amy Milton came in the
day after with a rumour about Katy and Max and everyone was
talking. I knew she wouldn't have cos she was my best friend.

But Amy kept on –

It's true
They went into Siobhan's parents' upstairs bathroom
They were in there for 20 minutes
Siobhan was knocking on the door because she needed to puke
But they didn't come out

I was seething. Wounded. My lip nearly went.
When I saw her at lunch, I knew it was true
I didn't say anything and she didn't either
I couldn't think, I couldn't focus on lessons
Neither could the other me
Last period we had History and she passed me a note
– *R u ok ?*
I scrunched it up.
After the lesson she handed me a long letter.
I pocketed it. Ignored her. Legged it to the locker room
Grabbed my bag, got out of there quick as I could
Reeling all the way home
I felt sick.
Bile in my gut.
In retrospect I was in love
As much in love as a fourteen year old can be
Which to be fair, is simultaneously complete nonsense and also
totally and utterly all-encompassingly intense and <u>true</u>.
It was also my absolute duty to deny this publicly and privately
To any and all who accused me of fancying her

I *do not*. She's my best friend

Yeah but it's obvious

Yeah but I *don't*. Fuck you.

But I did.
Obviously.
It was obvious to the world probably.
To her, probably.
She could have chosen any other guy in school and it would
have been fine
Honestly, it would have been fine if it was any other guy

Beat.

They started going out.
Fuck, that's a lie
They weren't going out –
They were fucking about.
I was betrayed
Or that's how it felt.
I know *now* she didn't betray me
But at fourteen, it's betrayal
And I knew it –
I knew it –
I knew he would do this –
A few weeks later
He fucked her over
Went around the common room
Telling everyone

I tongued her mate
Grabbed myself a handful of tit
Fingered her didn't I
Here – smell these
I'm done with her
She's a frigid slut
She's got a terrible face
She mings
No arse, no chat
Awful breath
Doesn't matter as long as it's on my cock –

Cunt.

He *bragged* and belittled her
To the whole common room
I sat in the corner
While everyone laughed

Beat.

A few weeks later at lunch
I saw her sat on a bench
I saw she was hurting.

But I couldn't talk to her
I stopped speaking to her, cold.

Pause.

Last day of term, breaking up for the summer
she wrote me a letter, gel-pen pink

Hey
I wish we could talk. I'm not really sure what I did wrong.
Please speak to me. I thought about calling you loads of times
but I wasn't sure if you were pissed at me. Actually I know
you're pissed at me, but I don't know why. My mum even asked
why you hadn't called the house for ages. It's making me so
sad. We've been through too much to let anyone else stop us
being friends. I don't want to lose you. I think even if you stay
mad at me for a while you won't be forever because I really
think – I *know* – we'll be friends forever. I really care about
you. So much. I really miss you. I can't imagine not speaking
to you. You're my best friend. I miss you more than anything. I
just wish you'd talk to me again.

He breaks off.

I never replied.

Beat.

not, I think, out of spite
but because of what happened
in the summer holidays

*

We were going to see my Aunt in Montréal. I loved going to
the airport. McDonalds for breakfast. I badgered my Dad to let
me buy a new pair of headphones for my Walkman. Panasonic
or JVC. Couldn't afford Sony. Head down, running to Dixons.
I was wrenched back, my arm almost yanked out of its socket.
This hulking figure in black uniform stood over me, weapon
ready.

Where are you going?
Where are you going?
Where are you travelling to?

I was suddenly aware that if I didn't give the right answer
He might shoot me dead
I was a child
I was scared

Pause.

He stared me up and down.
Dug his fingers into my arm
Marched me along the terminal
In front of all the other passengers
Disappeared me through a security door
The other me wanted to cry
Although my throat was bursting
I did not let him out.

Pause.

People who kill don't look like me
People who hit women don't look like me
They look like Max.
And his dad.
That's profiling.
There's your killer
Profile *them.*

Beat.

They put me in the scanner
Inspected my insides in 3D

Took me to a room
And left me there.

Where's your boarding pass?

I don't

Show me your boarding pass

My Dad's got my boarding pass

What's your flight number?

I don't know

The number of your flight

I don't

Gate?

I don't know

You don't know where you're flying to?

I –

Where?

Canada –
Canada –
My Auntie lives in Canada

Pause.

He looked at me indifferent
Stared for a long time

You were acting suspicious
You're lucky

He left me in the airport lounge
as if nothing had ever happened.
I slunk back to mum and dad.
Dad was stressed because I'd taken so long
They were waiting to go to the gate

Did you get what you wanted?

Yeah

I sat in silence, sank into myself

Hid tears
Didn't say a word about what'd happened
And from then on
I wasn't a kid anymore
I carried fear in my soul
I wasn't allowed to be a lost little boy
I wasn't allowed to be the one in trouble
I wasn't a victim
I was a suspect
I was a threat.

Pause.

*

Back to school – September, Year 11
PE. Changing rooms. Before lunch.
Max and me – it was arranged in maths
A note passed down; he wants a fight.
The bell went and everyone emptied out
I didn't want to hit him, I didn't see the point
I let him put me in a headlock
Didn't know what to do
He kneed me in the head –

I knew you wouldn't do anything
Pussy
You're obsessed with Katy.
What's wrong with you?
You're gay anyway
You fucking freak
She's a loser,
She's got fat thighs, she's a slut.
She'd get off with anyone
Except for you –

Pause.

I went mad – hit the cunt – punched him in the eye
His nose bent backwards like it was made of clay
He looked back, stunned, tears welling
Shocked myself, didn't dare to hit him again
A pink spot of blood speckled his PE shirt
Then a deep scarlet trickle onto the floor
I could taste iron in my mouth.
He ran out.
That was that.
But when I came out they were all there
Outside the changing rooms
Him and his mates.
Fuck.

They yanked my backpack off my back
Dragged me down by my blazer
Max kicked the wind out of my lungs
Split my shirt and ripped the buttons off
Stamped me in the nuts
So hard I couldn't breathe

Yo Osama
What's in your bag
Get to Guantanamo, Taliban cunt

They launched my rucksack into the bushes.
Max was grinning.
He stepped on my skull
Held the pressure
Til I thought
My jaw would crack

Silence.

*

End of the year. School trip. Natural History Museum. Me and
Katy hadn't said a word to each other. We always used to sit
together at the back of the coach and listen to music. I'd make
her a playlist. We'd have a headphone each and share the song in
our heads. This time I sat with Harry. He picked his nose. The
whole day was washed out by a storm.

Waiting for the coach home
We got caught in the rain
Me and Katy sheltered under the bus stop, side by side.
After a minute
She offered me a headphone.
I took it – she grabbed me and I grabbed her back
Skin pressed up against each other's
Her cheek on mine, freezing cold
She put her numb hand in mine
I held it tight, squeezed the blood back in
We held onto each other for an eternity, breathless.
The next day she came up to me in the quad
Thought we were right again,

Part of me was desperate to say sorry –
I *wanted to* – I *wanted to* – I *wanted to*
But I couldn't get his face out of my head.

PART II

THE CITY

4. PTSD

Awake. 4am.
Sudden rain.
Teeth bared
Two yellow eyes
Pierce the dark.
Someone is stood
at the bedroom door.
Unmoving, silent
He melted
Out the room
And I was unstuck.
I got out of bed
Followed
No one there.
I looked out the window
Along Seven Sisters Road
Calm, quiet, no cars passing.
In a pool of light by the lampposts
A foal, alone in the road.

Pause.

22.
I lived in the city
In a shit flat with my friend Robyn
When we looked round the first time
She immediately knew it was shit
She cornered the Estate Agent

It smells of gas – can you smell that?

I swear to you, *swear down* yeah –
I ain't never smelled that smell before.

It smells like a gas leak.

Yeah, yeah, yeah to be fair yeah
I see what you're saying yeah
Yeah we should get the gas checked.

<u>The flat didn't *have gas.*</u>
The night we got the keys
We got pizza from across the road
It was shit
It was *delicious*
It was everything
I walked at night
The city held me
It was alive
It was dangerous
It rained
It was a dream

The neighbours were nice. Two Polish women who hung about in tracky b's and vest tops. We got on well, chatted in the hallway. They never seemed to go out very much. Over the next few months it slowly dawned on me that they were prostitutes and the flat upstairs was a brothel. I got a text from Robyn once late at night

Don't come home
What?
If you can stay somewhere else tonight, don't come home – the whole street's closed
R u joking?
The whole street has been cordoned off by the police.

I crashed at a mate's, came back the next morning
The whole road was sealed off with tape
I wandered through to our front door
Policemen swarming through the cornershop
They'd raided it – thought it was a weed factory
Found a Meth Lab instead.
Had to shut off the whole street in case it blew up.

In retrospect, I should have noticed. I had only been in there once – they didn't have any toilet roll and they had Custard

Creams from 1995. *Odd*, I thought. Not – this is a meth lab. But you want to give people the benefit of the doubt. Winter came. Our ceiling leaked directly onto a plug socket and when we turned the heating on it sparked. So I slept in a sleeping bag under the duvet, fully clothed; hat and gloves. Frost on the windows. Single glazed. Barely glazed. It was a shit flat. But at least I'd got off the Island.

Pause.

I barely spoke to my parents. My sister did her own thing. I didn't know her anymore. We weren't in touch. I didn't speak to anyone from home, the odd text from Harry. I knew Katy had moved to the city but we didn't speak. I looked different. Lost the puppy fat. I didn't miss the sea. But I wasn't the same as the city people. I was an *Islander*. Apparently, it's weird to call it The Mainland. When people found out I was from the Island they would be like – oh my god do you know Bryony Hollingsworth?? Why would I know her?! That's just a random name you're saying. As it happens, we did actually go to the same nursery so in that instance *yes* – I do know her. But – . I didn't know anyone in the city. In the city I could *walk around* and no one would *notice* me. I was no one. A stray.

Pause.

The song in my head would sing me to sleep
But I would always wake at 4 a.m.
The night never silent
I couldn't sleep with the door closed
So I kept it open, the doorway a portal
To another place; dark black
Creeping dread
A feeling in the back of my head
That someone, some creature
Was about to burst in
Catch me defenceless
Attack me as I slept
His presence was there
I could *feel him*
A shadow, ascending

to the ceiling
Hanging over me
Decaying wings of a dead bird
Talons curled like claws
Ready to cut my throat
So I stayed awake.
Bowl of cereal
Midnight Shreddies
Listened to the birds at first light
Drifted off as their song brought the sun
Fell into some fitful dream.

*

Silence.

At school I got rejected from every single retail job. Must have been something to do with my personality. Last chance was The Admiral, a pub on the seafront. All the rejects worked there including Harry. If you applied you were guaranteed a job behind the bar. I got an interview, piece of piss. Turned up for my first day, the manager walked me upstairs, handed me a set of whites and pushed open the doors to the kitchen. The Head Chef stood there holding this big fuck-off knife –

Chop the salad.

How?

He looked at me like I was a prick.
I was.
I had no idea what I was doing or why I was there.

The best utensil to butter your bread with is a – ?
Spoon, you cunt.

Beat.

It was a mashup of people from all over, older guys from Zimbabwe, Hong Kong, kids from Southsea, Havant, Emsworth, out of catering college, all under the Head Chef Andy, who would relentlessly tell everyone he wasn't racist.

How can I be?
My sister's married to a black man

Black as the ace of spades
So how's it that I'm racist?
Impossible
Plus, I got a black dog.

Pause.

Once you've got a job in a kitchen
You can always get a job in a kitchen.
So that's what I did when I got to the city.
(Which, obviously, brought shame upon the family)
I found artfulness in food; I loved the pace, the precision
The heat of the stove, the salamander
It was fast and it was fucking hard
And it was money and it was grit and grime
Hard graft under fluorescent lights
Which gave me a splitting headache.

After work I'd walk along the river
Sit on the shore
Let the nausea subside
The water was muddy, murky
You could drown in it, and nobody would find you
And who would care
I found it peaceful, in a way, thinking about that
I felt I could see them
Sunk bodies of those who were lost
Forgotten, dead or murdered
I'd watch the water, get some air back into my lungs
And then it was back in the morning
Rewind repeat.

Pause.

*

I saw Max twice in the city
Once on the street, in Soho
He was taller, grown into himself
Shiny suit plastic tie, still did his hair with too much gel
He came round the corner, walked into me

Oh my god, alright mate?
What you upto, you live here?

He stank of Lynx
I figured he was a property manager or some meaningless shit
He luxuriated in smugness, wore a horrible grin
He put out his hand to shake
As I went to take it, he pulled it away –

Smell ya later!

And then he fucked off.
Can you fucking believe that?
Classless cock.

Pause.

After I saw him, I was headed to the tube,
Head somewhere else, in a haze –
An old lady stopped me in the station

You better not run like that

What?

You had better not *run*

I'm sorry?

With a backpack on –
I wouldn't run down the escalator like that
If I were you
With a backpack on – looking like that.

?

What're those, headphones?
Looks like a *wire* sticking out.
D'you get me?
So you'd better not run like that
Someone might think you're one from
Guantanamo Bay
You know?
You saw they shot that one?
Jumped the barrier

Running like you
They shot him in the head, did you see?

Pause.

I did see. I dreamed it. I imagined another me sat on the tube done nothing wrong. Thinking about what song to choose on my mp3 player. And then *BAM* my brains are on the walls and windows. Splattered over the people sat beside me.

Pause.

So are you gonna run or are you gonna walk?

I've gotta get my train.

Pause.

Shall I get them
Shall I go get them?

What?

Shall I go get them now?
If you're gonna run.
I'll go get them, shall I?
See what they'll do.

She started laughing, old bat.
Like the wicked witch of the west.
I walked slowly to the platform.
Eyes down, headphones in.
Pretended I didn't care.

Pause.

3 a.m.
Thunderstorm
The other me
With his head blown apart
Leans over
Pushes down on my chest
His other hand
Covers my face
Won't let me breathe

Feels like he's trying
To pull my ribcage apart
Tetanus
Limbs locked
Rictus grin
Sinews taut
I know I have to wake up
I will myself to wake
Force my eyes open
But my body doesn't move
He asks me
How can I save my soul?
What am I supposed to say?
On the banks of the river I crawl through clay
I gasp for breath
Rain pours

5. Dogs // Donkeys

The streets were getting filthy – rancid, full of litter. I didn't speak much, didn't go out except to work. Downward spiral. A few weeks later Harry came to visit. He'd dropped out of uni, moved back home, got in touch out of the blue. Said he needed to get off the Island for a bit. He looked the same. He was pencil-thin, wore the same skate clothes as when we were kids. He loped around the flat like old spaghetti. Smoking rollies out of the window. I think he came to cheer me up.

The Island should be sunk into the sea
It's full of wankers
I'm serious
Although to be fair
The city is full of even bigger wankers, so…
Glad I didn't move here

He stared out the window
Dripping ash onto his shirtsleeve

I'm in a bit of trouble mate
Got stupidly addicted to heroin
Sold all my music gear
Owe a bit of money.
Tony Barnes, Gary Grindle.
Probably break my nose.
Actually, to be fair
They've got a place up here
South London haven't they
Snooker club
Probably find me anyway…

Beat.

Hey, you should move back to the Island
We can take over the donkey sanctuary
Hang out with the donkeys
They're just
They're just lovely aren't they
Lovely guys, donkeys, aren't they
I love them, donkeys.
Underrated.
I think in the future
They should give the world back
To dogs and donkeys
Let them be in charge
Because they're kind.
How's your mum?

Pause.

*

Mum was…
Mum was –

Why do you never call?
Why do you never speak to us?
Why do we never speak?
You don't want to talk to us
You don't want to know how we are
You don't want to know.

I admit. There was the desire to go back. Every so often. It's
as if there's a sort of *need* to go home. But once you get there.
You have to immediately leave. The sea has a gravitational
pull. I don't think people appreciate how loud it is. You yield
to it. Your head empties. So I went back sometimes. Expecting
something different each time. But every time the same:

Why aren't you more like your sister?
She calls us every week.
She comes to visit.
Why have you
Why do you
Are you taking care of your teeth?
Don't wear dark clothes, it will make you look dark
Are you losing your hair?
Honestly, it makes me sick
You have put on weight
What do you eat?
Why don't you earn enough money?
Why aren't you doing well?
Why haven't you made something of yourself?
You never will
What do you *do? – Make food?*
Who's going to want to eat it?
Making food is an act of generosity
But you don't have an ounce of generosity in you
You make food for people, for *family* –
But how can you make food for other people
When you don't understand them?
You'll always be alone
Because if anyone gets close to you
They'll *see* you
They'll be scared of you.
Like I am.

Pause.

So no I didn't really want to go home to be honest with you

Beat.

Dad text me,
All caps
RING US
I didn't
COME HOME
I did not

Go home?
Why would I go home?
Go home why?
Go home and be judged
Go home and be bullied?
Go home and be scrutinised for every fucking thing
Go home and be told that every decision you've ever made is
wrong
Go home and be taunted and picked on and mocked and
undermined
And told you're a waste
And told you're worthless
Go home why?

Pause.

He texted again
RING NOW

Pause.

You have to come home
Mum is not feeling very safe
We were walking along the seafront
And your mum noticed these boys were following us
You know what they shouted?
Pakis go home.
I said –
We live up the hill, we will go home.
So, we went on our way – they kept following
I knew the boy who shouted –
He went to your school
Very tall boy

I knew who he was on about – Liam Grindle
Lanky cunt like his twat father.

This sort of thing has happened to us for 30 years
You think it bothers me?
But Mum is feeling unhappy
The next morning, I came outside to water the plants
They had pulled up all the roses
Ripped out the roots
At least I won't have to tend to the garden anymore.

He was making a joke
But I could hear his voice shaking
And clearly – he wanted to tell me
Because he wanted me to *do something*
Still, I did not come.

Pause.

Finally,
He text again

Mum is sick.
Do you care?

Pause.

Mum was always sick
She'd be fine.
Always complaining
Always had an ailment or an illness
It'd be nothing
She'd get better
It'd be fine.

But Dad persisted
Texted again
Mum's feeling anxious
She doesn't want to go outside
She's forgetting her English
What's that got to do with me?
Why can't you talk to her?
Why did you never learn Hindi?

Because you never fucking taught me
It's no wonder we don't speak
We don't speak the same fucking language.

Silence.

Another text
Unknown number
Hey how are you doing?
New phone, who dis?
I chucked the phone on my bed
It's *Katy*.

Beat.

New phone who dis? You dick.

Do you live in the city?
Would you want to meet up?
I've been thinking about you
I just thought of you and
I wanted to see how you were

– I'd thought about her every day since we met

Beat.

I waited by Hammersmith bridge
Sifting through the faces
Wondering what she looked like now
Wondering if she'd recognise me

Pause.

Hey.

Hey.

She was smiling
I must have smiled back
Because she smiled at me even harder
And gave me a hug
I must have hugged back
Because what else would you do
I wish I could have held onto that moment

Her arms around me, tight
But it was gone and we were walking
And the night was cold

6. He fell to his death

They beat a boy to death. South of the city. It was a burning
Winter's day. Things were fractious, fragile. A hate march
metastasised through the city. I walked past them in Trafalgar
Square, thugs draped in the St. George's Cross. They'd come
from all over the country. Bare pink bellies, stinking of piss and
booze, waving flags from fountains with their home towns and
factions. The night bred violence. They attacked a hotel housing
asylum seekers, set a police van on fire. Hoods and balaclavas,
bricks and metal.

Pause.

The boy was nothing to do with anything
He was just a kid coming home from school, 13

A group from the rally followed him and his mates
They said it was the boys provoking them
Lobbing stones and making threats.
He got separated from his friends
And instead of following the group
They followed him
He tried to ignore them, walked on
Weaved his way in and out of the smaller streets
But they kept on his tail, wouldn't let it go
He turned a corner and started to run.
They bolted after him, scenting fear
Rabid, frothing, they ran him down
Cornered, he climbed up a fire escape
the pack beneath, baying for blood

Pause.

He fell from the metal staircase
Hit his head on the pavement;
He died in hospital
after a few weeks of being in a coma.
But it wasn't the fall that killed him
He was beaten after he fell
They attacked him when he was helpless, hurt
And left him there to die.

Beat.

His mum went on TV; she seemed so calm
I didn't know how she could be so dignified
She asked the world if they knew what had happened
If anyone knew the truth.
The police appealed for witnesses
But no one came forward.
They questioned a few
Members of a group
But they all stayed quiet
And no one was charged.

Silence.

They showed a picture of him
On the news
Asian boy
He looked like me
At first it didn't really register
Nothing to do with me.
But beneath
There set a fire

Pause.

*

Katy and I had been going out for a few months. It didn't seem
real. We reconnected. Found common ground. Digression:
Women and People of Colour. We're in the same boat. The
Alliance. Okay, resume: Katy and I walked, wandered. Made
friends with the night. We went on little quests to find the best
coffee, best *hot chocolate*. One night we were looking for the

best *croquetas*. We found a Spanish restaurant where at some
level we knew some of the people there were twats but we had
to honour the quest. The croquetas were class. Katy fiddled with
a calamari ring.

Do you want kids?

Of course not –
I wouldn't bring a little boy into this
I couldn't protect him.
This?
It would be mad.

How do you know it would be a him?
It could be a her.
Or twins.

No way.
There's no way.
How?
I can't afford it.
I don't have any money.
I don't have a mortgage.
I'm not gonna have a house.
I'm not gonna have a pension.

Can you imagine yourself as a father?

Me?
I couldn't look after a child.
There's no way – What about a dog?

Pause.

I looked up expecting to see her laugh but
I caught disappointment
That's when he appeared
The second time I saw him –
Max.

Pause.

He dragged over a chair, uninvited
Scraped up to our table

Helped himself to a fistful of patatas bravas
Grinning; he stank of aperol
Dipped his greasy fingers in our little bowl of water

Alright cunts?

He looked at the two of us together
And started to howl with laughter

Don't tell me...
You two?
The two of you?
No way!
Are you serious?
Love's young dream?

He popped an olive in his mouth
I hoped he'd choke

It's so mad to see you both
Kate you're looking good

Katy wasn't bothered by him
Insulated by her intelligence
She gave him a look which made his dick shrink
And excused herself, repulsed.

Oooh – come on now.
What did I say?...

He looked me up and down
He had aioli on his jacket

Did you know we fucked?

He reached over, downed my Rioja.
Slunk off back to his slimy mates
Or at least that's what I thought
I felt like I was a child again
Couldn't move, couldn't speak
Timid, helpless.

After about ten minutes, Katy came back
Shaken, she wanted to leave

What happened?

He followed me

What?

He followed me into the toilets
He cornered me
Up against the cubicle

He what?
What did he do?

He –
It doesn't matter

What the *fuck* did he do?

He didn't do anything.
He just –
He just tried to…
He was just being
He's drunk
He's –
You know what he's like
He just was talking shit
He was being an ass
Honestly, it's okay.
Can we –

We stood outside, two kids in the rain holding hands
Clinging onto each other for dear life

Pause.

I was fuming
As we walked to the station
My phone rang –
I never have it on loud
But somehow it still rang.
Sometimes the phone rings a different ring
And you know something has happened.
It was my sister
Not now. Leave me alone.

Put it in my pocket
Tried to stay in that moment
Stay with Katy
She knew something was up
I shrugged it off
When we got back to mine
She made me a cup of tea
Held my hand
We lay there curled up
Breathing slowly
Breathing slow
My phone buzzed again

Shouldn't you pick up?

No, not now
It's late

It's fine – get it,
it's important

Hit silent
But it rang again

I think something's happening
With my mum

Then you should get it

No – I'm not picking up

Text from my sister
You should come now
It was obvious that I should have
That anyone else would
But I didn't want to speak to them
I couldn't tell her why
I couldn't explain
I couldn't express
How painful it is to go back
That I was scared
I didn't want to call

I didn't want to go back
I didn't know how to tell her
That they hurt me
They crush me
They stop me from breathing

I don't care what happens.
I don't care.
I don't *care*.

Pause.

Katy was looking at me

I knew something had changed
I'd let her see who I was
She'd seen inside
She'd seen the terrible part of me
In a second I knew it was ruined
She knew I was selfish, callous, unkind
She slipped out of the duvet
Listen, I should go.
You should speak to your Mum and Dad.
Maybe you need to go back to the Island.

I'll go, I will go
I'll go tomorrow
I'm tired
I'll phone later
Just, right now
I can't
I want us
I want to stay here
I feel safe here
This is special
Us

I have to go

You don't understand
Please
Mercy.

Please stay with me
Please.

Silence.

She closed the door calmly
Her footsteps echoed down the staircase
And I was left alone
Quietly shattering inside
I suddenly knew *I would have with her*
I realised what she was asking in the restaurant and
I would have with her,
I could imagine it with her
I wanted to tell her
But it was too late
Lump in my throat
My lip quivered
Until it split into a thousand fragments
Each splintered piece spinning into space
My skull imploding; a dying star
The other me – him
The echo of me
implored me to talk
wanted to teach me something
About compassion
About being caring
He wanted to cry
The *coward*
I tried to strangle the thought
Hand on his throat
Pressed on his neck
So hard
Until
– pop –
My vision cracked
Split down the middle
Zigzag stripes cut across my iris
Neon yellow curdling against black
A cracked LCD screen leaking RGB colour
Light blooming into a halo

Head burning
Like it had been cleaved in two
I sat on the floor in the dark
Face in my hands
Black fluid leaking from my eyes
Soaking into my sheets
Like ink

Silence.

In the morning I had a voicemail
My sister, in tears
She's gone
She went this morning
You should have come
You should have called
You caused her a lot of pain.

Silence.

I was going to go.

Silence.

I would have gone.

Silence.

I didn't go outside for days
didn't speak to a soul
pouring rain,
paralysed in bed
over and over
Her voice

You are a failure
You are a failure
You are a failure
You are a failure

Pause.

I think I am asleep.

Pause.

Eyes open
He is stood at the door
His eyes pierce the dark
He hangs over me, melting black
Waiting to consume me
He let in the night
Maybe it was him; the someone else
who wants to wear my skin
Panic; heart pounding in my chest
Blood drains from my arm
And it falls limp
I am sinking into sand
My head is filled with worms, caterpillars
Red admiral butterflies burst out of my skull

PART III

HOME

7. Endgame

With no doubt in my mind
It would be better if we left this earth
If we ceded control
Relinquished our dominion
Brought back wolves, let them loose in the city
Cause carnage; maybe things would be quieter, calmer
I would happily wait for the Tsunami
Be washed away

Silence.

33.
Around this time there was a terrible incident at work
A maître d' asked me
Why are you always so negative?
I said – Look outside, it's raining.
He said – So what? It's raining – That doesn't make any sense.
I said – How *dare you*
How can you expect me to make sense when the world makes
no sense?
He looked at me like I was a fucking cunt.
That's when the incident happened –
And *I was asked to leave?*

Silence.

One night I got a message from Harry.
A photo of his ear dripping in blood
Followed by a stream of texts

I've just been at a lock-in with Max's Dad and his mates
They were on a bender mad on crack

Dicks out like they owned the place
Rob Dixon starts bragging
About this group he's in
Some skinhead crew
Says they got this network
Around the country, getting bigger
And he's some big deal in it
He goes on about how they beat up this boy
Years ago, in the city
The others were like – shut the fuck up
But he was like – so what?
Little prick fell off the wall, it was his own fault.
Said he kicked him in the neck
Said they all did, all had a go
Said he played his best round of snooker ever afterwards
Shot his best break
Everyone laughed, the punters in the room
Pissheads, cokeheads, I don't think they believed it
Grindle was like nah nah they're just joking
But Max's Dad looked nervous –
Dixon was like don't worry no one's gonna end up in Parkhurst
Over a little paki humpty dumpty fell off a wall
It was like he was confessing 'cept it wasn't a confession
They were talking about it out in the open
Max saw me – he knew I'd heard.
He came over with his Dad and Rob and they were like
Let's go outside for a minute
They said if I said anything
They'd kick my fucking head in
I said obviously I wouldn't say anything, I promised
The others were like alright, they left it
But Max's Dad hanged back,
He was off his nut
Eyes were crazy
He put a Stanley knife to my neck
Cut my ear
He said if I say anything to anyone
He'll kill me
But I'm literally breaking that promise right now

Silence.

I went outside
Couldn't breathe
Gut twisted

Beat.

When I was a kid
My parents said – *they said* – be careful
They're out there after you
BNP, National Front
I said – you're <u>wrong</u>
That doesn't exist anymore
That doesn't happen now

Pause.

Thirteen years old
That boy ran
In fear for his life
An act of terror.

Pause.

The sea called.
A thought came
So clearly into my skull
The rain isn't gonna come
and wash the bad people away

*

I looked out the window
Along Seven Sisters Road
Two eyes reflect the light
A Foal
Black coat, sleek like oil
Lost in the middle of the road
I walk towards it
Jaw locked
Teeth ground tight

Pause.

Ripped from my sleep
Eyes to the ceiling
Couldn't move
I could feel His fingernails
Scratching at the inside of my ribcage
Forcing their way out of my chest
I felt the first tendon snap
Back arched, eyeballs bulging
He began to shatter my bones
Split them into shards
I felt my cells tearing apart
He held me down
Pushed on my chest
Peeled himself away
Shedding a skin
He crawled out of me
The shadow –
That was when I split in two.

8. Ghost

Leaving the city, I felt lost. I was a ghost. At Waterloo station I
had a sad Pret. Burned my tongue on my tea. The train dragged
through the countryside. Grey gave way to green. The smell
of the sea hit a few stops from the harbour. I thought I was
going back a stranger, but as I waited at The Hard the ferry man
stopped me

Didn't you get the ferry before?

Sorry, what?

Weren't you on the ferry before?

Pause.

I've just got déjà vu, mush –
Thought I'd seen you before

I know you don't I
You used to get the boat when you were a nipper
Went over to Gunwharf with your mates

I nodded.
Maybe it was the other me he'd recognised
I bought my ticket (fucking extortionate)
Boarded the ferry
Unhappy crossing
The waves were rough
The boat bashed against the pier
As we docked unsteady
I felt nauseous, bothered
Walking up the esplanade
The wind battered me
I watched
A mother and her foal
Dancing on the beach
The old shops were still there
The arcade
Time moves differently

Pause.

I found out from facebook that Katy had moved back. She had
three kids, quit her job as an architect. Husband, family, a house
in Lake. I thought about going to see her, knocking on her
door. We'd sit in the back garden, eat mint choc chip ice cream.
Delusional. As if she would care. Maybe he'd go – the other
me.

Pause.

I went home. Trudged up the hill. Stood at the end of the
driveway. The flower beds were grown over with weeds and
moss. I didn't even know if my key would work. But the lock
clicked open. I slipped inside. It felt mad somehow, unreal.
Everything was still there, sofas, Dad's old chair. Dirty dishes
out on the side, Encona Hot Sauce on the table. I thought about
calling upstairs. I wanted to go up with a glass of hot ribena.
Sit by his bed and hold his hand. But Dad wouldn't have

understood who I was now. Half a person. Shattered in two. I
rummaged around, stalked the house like a spectre.

I wondered where the fuck he'd put mum.
On the mantelpiece maybe
Or maybe she was gone, scattered in the sea
I dunno what I was looking for
A fucking urn or something I dunno

As I searched, I heard a sound from the spare room
Music, on the piano. I pushed through the door
There, sat on the piano stool, playing softly,
the most beautiful piece – there he was:
The Other.
Wearing my hoodie, and my skin.
Without stopping, he spoke.

What ferry did you get?

Uh…
The 4.20

Oh that's so funny, I was on the 3.20
We almost got the same ferry.

Silence.

Why did you never practise?

I beg your pardon?

You were good, but you never practised.
Why did you never try harder?
What a waste.

He stared at me with my eyes.

Pause.

Don't go up and see him
Don't
Don't bother him
Don't hurt him

Hurt him?

Hurt him? Me?
I protected them.
I protect them.
I protect.
What do *you* do?
You're weak.
Scared.

He stopped playing.

Silence.

There's some post for you

He handed me a pile of letters, all addressed to me –
Junk, bank statements, student loan stuff
And underneath them,
A stack of envelopes, handwritten, all from Mum.
Maybe Dad figured I'd come home one day
Pick up my mail.

I should go up –

Don't.

I –

Do better.

Pause.

I opened one, ripped off the top
It said –

Feeling Sad.

Something has upset me. Our friend Pam is dying. She has
cancer of the pancreas. Pam's children have come home from
the Mainland to support her. We will die soon too on this Island,
alone. No help from our children. In our old age I thought we
would get love and support from you but I was wrong. You
turned out to be a different person from the one I expected.
You aren't who I imagined. You used to be caring. Where was
the loving little boy who used to want me to read him stories?
Perhaps he never existed. I have decided that I want our

relationship to end. I have had enough of the hatred you direct at me. It would be better if you stay away. I am useless to you anyway. Don't come back.

Mum.

Silence.

I went out into the night.
The trees were electric
Ecstatic with light
I walked up the road to Max's
It didn't take long
The yard was still full of the same old junk
Broken masonry and bashed up patio chairs
Through the windows I could see lights inside
Some kind of gathering, a film on TV
Outside in the rain chained to a railing
A huge black dog; bull mastiff
He looked at me with those eyes
Deep and soulful
Didn't bark
Didn't bite
I knew he wouldn't
Maybe he knew I was there to do some good
He let me walk right up to the front step.

Pause.

I found myself fixed to the floor, paralysed
A scared child, courage drained out of me
Pathetic, fucking coward; *stop being afraid*
I forced my limbs to move; *move you fucker*
And before I'd had a chance to think I'd rung the bell.

Beat.

Max opened the door.
He was standing right there; the cunt didn't recognise me.
I hit him in the face with a hammer
He seemed shocked, staggered back
It left a hole

Scarlet and black
Could see his incisors through his face
I was surprised at myself, pleased
Calm
No frenzy
I grabbed him by the neck
gripped his windpipe
Dug my fingers into his throat
Felt his arteries bulge
Breath constrict
I showed mercy
Let him go, gasping for air
He fell on the floor asphyxiating
I watched him struggle, stepped over him
Wandered down the corridor into the front room.
It stank of lager, sweat, and pork cracklings
His Dad and two others, beer bellies hanging out of their shirts
Sat round a table; late night poker party –
Jackie Chan movie on – Police Story maybe.
I recognized Gary Grindle and his stupid face
Rob Dixon was beside him, adidas cap, hoodie, tats   They
looked at me startled, almost laughed
Couldn't believe what they were seeing
Who the fuck are you?
Another one I didn't know came out the loo reeking of piss
Horrible-looking troll, like a bowl of rancid chicken
He took one look at me
Stuttered out – f-fucking paki – do you know this one?
And then they noticed the hammer stained in blood.

Sidebar:
Paki –
It's never made sense.
It's never hurt.
They sling it at you
But I don't get it –
> I'm not from Pakistan <
It doesn't describe me
It doesn't fit

They try *all the others*
The ones that don't belong to me
They make even less sense
They hurt even less
You fucking cretin
At least be accurate
At least work out *who you're trying to abuse*
You've got the wrong word
The word is wrong
Master of your own language?
You can't speak it – I can.
I don't think you *have* a word
You can't describe me
You don't have a word for me
There is no word for me

Pause.

4-against-1
They came at me, crammed along the corridor
I smacked Grindle away, he wasn't a fighter, slunk off into the corner
Big Rob stuck his fat thumbs round my throat
I swung into the wall, shook him off, hit him hard
He went down unmoving
Good, I thought
Then the other one stabbed me in the neck
Fuck I thought, that's an issue
I think the adrenaline hit because I felt fine
But as I picked myself up
Max launched at me
Out of the shadows
I smashed him in the face
He spat out red
Three teeth in a scarlet puddle
He fell to the floor confused
Bone and muscle
Splitting, splintering
He stopped shouting
And everything was silent

Max's Dad was sweating
Panting in the doorway
He looked scared
Good, I thought
I think he was having a heart attack

You *fucking animal*
Take whatever you want

He'd missed the point.

Pause.

The scene before me was like some baroque painting
They were writhing around like garden slugs
At this precise point I stopped caring
About what might happen to them
Or what would happen to me.
I remember thinking
Well,
We all die sometime
What matters is whether you did something good
Were you kind?
Did you do good?
Did you do your best?

Silence.

I walked back into the yard
Cold rain.
Puddles forming on the concrete patio
I let the dog off his chain
He licked my hand
Looked up at me
Big beautiful eyes
Put my arm round his head
Gave him a scratch
His hot wet tongue slathered on my ear
Kindness not cruelty;
I learned that from a sticker on our car.
I looked back at the house
Max's feet were poking out round the side of the door
Like a comedy pair of legs in a film.

I sat down, propped up against the gate
I was warm
I didn't feel a thing
I felt happy.

He smiles.

Pause.

The rain pooled on the ground
I realised I was getting a wet bum.
I took out the letters from my pocket
Started to read them one by one
The last one looked recent
I tried not to get blood on it
At the top it said

Mum's Advice.

My handsome boy. I know you will not like to hear this. I know you will not like to listen to us, especially your Mother but I want you to take my advice. As your Mother I know what is correct and what is not. Your skin is dry and your scalp is oily. In this respect, you are like your Father. Please make sure that you have no unsightly hair showing, like ear hair and nose hair. If you do, get rid of it. You can use a tweezer for the nose. If you live with another person or ever have a special friend, do not go for the biggest portion. Let other people help themselves first. Otherwise it will give the impression that you are greedy and selfish. Always try to listen patiently to others who have views different from yours. There may be points you didn't consider before. Do not be aggressive in putting your views forward. I know that will be a particular problem for you. Please try to be good this year.

For now, this will be all.

Always remember I love you very much.

Silence.

I looked up.
The sky started to change

9. CODA

I staggered down the path to the shore
Thoughts falling out of my cracked head
Indigo gave way to the first flecks of pink
Black blood danced on the sand

Silence.

Don't whimper
In a corner
Bite
Bark
Hit back
Resist
I won't be bullied
I won't submit
Threaten me I will rip at your throat
I will break your spirit
I will ruin your life
Spit on me I'll skin you alive
I'll hunt you
I'll run you down
Muzzle *me*?
You can't.
You can't.
You scum
You cunt
You fuckhead
You will be scared
I know you're scared
Because I am the fucking future.
I am the future.
That's why you hate me.

Pause.

I *care*
I am made of care
I still am that little boy who cares
He never went away.

He never went anywhere.
I had to protect him
Me

Pause.

Corner an animal
Make him feel scared
That's when he's dangerous
Tell a creature he's a beast
One day he'll bite back

Pause.

I don't want to be scared anymore
I want to have hope
I want calm
I want a quiet mind
I want to undo myself
I want to be done
I want to be done
I want to be done.

Silence.

I thought about The Other Me. How when he let himself in the
house, he waited til the morning until Dad came down. The
next day they sat in the garden, talking, spending time together.
The sun came out. Blessed the rosebuds. They had a barbeque.
Dad got a text from my sister – she's getting the last ferry like
always. They'd all be together for a few days. Katy called.
Heard he was back on the Island. Knew his number off by heart.
He seemed happy. But he was still afraid. Maybe somewhere
inside he had the desire to do what I did. But he buried it
deep. Maybe he found a way for his dreams to be serene. And
all those things which had happened to him before, that had
made him scared, he took it all with good grace and learned to
forgive.

Pause.

Little foal
I searched day and night
To find you

I did well
I won the fight for you

Pause.

I sat by the sea
Waiting for sleep
Waiting for the sun to rise
I have this idea
You and me
The waves washed up
Seaweed and foam
I have this idea
Maybe I contain symphonies

End.

A Nick Hern Book

Foal first published in Great Britain as a paperback original in 2026 by Nick Hern Books Limited, The Glasshouse, 49a Goldhawk Road, London W12 8QP, in association with HFH Productions and the Finborough Theatre, London

Foal copyright © 2026 Titas Halder

Titas Halder has asserted his right to be identified as the author of this work

Cover image by Sari Soininen

Designed and typeset by Nick Hern Books, London
Printed in Great Britain by Mimeo Ltd, Huntingdon, Cambridgeshire PE29 6XX

A CIP catalogue record for this book is available from the British Library

ISBN 978 1 83904 584 4

www.nickhernbooks.co.uk/environmental-policy

Nick Hern Books' authorised representative in the EU is
Easy Access System Europe – Mustamäe tee 50, 10621 Tallinn, Estonia
email gpsr.requests@easproject.com